RACCOONS

NORTH AMERICAN ANIMAL DISCOVERY LIBRARY

Lynn M. Stone

Rourke Corporation, Inc.
Vero Beach, Florida 32964

PHOTO CREDITS

All photos by the author except: cover, pages 4, 15, 16 © Tom
and Pat Leeson

LIBRARY OF CONGRESS
Library of Congress Cataloging-in-Publication Data
Stone, Lynn M.
　　Raccoons / by Lynn M. Stone.

　　　p. cm. — (North American animal discovery library)
　　　Summary: An introduction to the physical characteristics,
habits, and natural environment of the raccoon.
　　ISBN 0-86593-045-7
　　1. Raccoons—Juvenile literature. [1. Raccoons.] I. Title.
II. Series: Stone, Lynn M. North American animal discovery
library.
QL737.C26S76　1990
599.74'443—dc20　　　　　89-70113
　　　　　　　　　　　　　　CIP
　　　　　　　　　　　　　　AC

Raccoons

TABLE OF CONTENTS

THE RACCOON

The raccoon *(Procyon lotor)* wears a black "mask" but is not a bandit. Actually, the raccoon's "mask" is just a handsome patch of black fur.

Bright eyes, a ringed tail, and thick fur make raccoons look much more cuddly than they are.

Raccoons have sharp teeth and claws. In battles between a dog and a raccoon, the much smaller raccoon can defend itself quite well.

Raccoons love water, and they are good swimmers. They are also good climbers.

Raccoon on fence

THE RACCOON'S COUSINS

The raccoon's closest cousins in North America are the ringtail and the coati.

Ringtails are **nocturnal** animals, just as raccoons are. Nocturnal animals are active at night.

Ringtails are found mostly in the southwestern states and Mexico.

The coati lives in Mexico and in corners of Texas, New Mexico, and Arizona. It has a long, pointed nose and a long, furry tail.

Unlike the raccoon and ringtail, the coati is busy during the day.

Coati in Arizona

HOW THEY LOOK

On the whole, raccoons are gray in color. A few are nearly black, and others have slightly red or even blond fur.

The raccoon has a fluffy tail with four to seven rings of dark fur.

Raccoons have sharp noses with black tips and long whiskers. They usually weigh from seven to 20 pounds. One old male, or **boar,** raccoon in Wisconsin fattened up to 62 pounds!

Raccoons measure from 24 to 37 inches in length.

Raccoon kit in Florida

WHERE THEY LIVE

Raccoons can be found throughout most of North America. That whole area is known as their **range.** They live across the United States except in some desert and mountain regions.

Raccoons also live in parts of Mexico and in southern Canada.

Raccoons seek out certain places within their range. These favorite places, the raccoons' homes, are called **habitats.**

Raccoons are usually found along streams or in swamps and marshes.

Some raccoons live in woodlands near large cities. These raccoons wander into backyards and gardens at night.

Raccoon in tree hollow

Raccoon kit on tree root

Raccoon kit

HOW THEY LIVE

Raccoons do most of their prowling at night when they look for food. Over several nights they may wander fairly far from where they began.

Raccoons have an amazing sense of touch in their front paws. They use their paws with great skill. Often a raccoon handles food and carefully dips it into water.

People once believed that raccoons were washing their food before eating it. Actually, raccoons just seem to enjoy handling food before eating it.

Raccoon in Northwest

THE RACCOON'S KITS

Raccoon babies are called **kits.** They are usually born in the spring.

A mother raccoon generally has four or five kits. Together they make up her **litter.**

Most baby raccoons are born in a tree hollow. Each weighs just two ounces.

Some young raccoons leave their mothers when they reach four months. Others spend the winter with their mothers.

Wild raccoons rarely live more than five years. Captive raccoons have lived to be 15.

Raccoon on branch

PREDATOR AND PREY

Because they eat plants and animals, raccoons are called **omnivores.** In the Latin language, "omni" means "all".

Raccoons are also **predators.** Predators are animals that hunt other animals. Raccoons feed on crayfish, frogs, baby muskrats, bird eggs, turtle eggs, and oysters, to name just a few.

They also eat seeds, ripe fruit, nuts, and garden crops. They have a special taste for corn.

Most larger animals don't attack full-grown raccoons. Young raccoons may be **prey,** or food, for eagles, hawks, owls, and bobcats.

Raccoon with frog

RACCOONS AND PEOPLE

Raccoons are cute, but wild raccoons are quick to snarl and bite.
Baby raccoons tame easily, and they make interesting, but messy, pets. They can open garbage pails, turn doorknobs, and even open refrigerators.
In the 1920s, raccoon coats were popular. Raccoon fur is still used in some women's clothing.
In autumn, raccoons are hunted in many places. The hunters follow the barks of their dogs until the raccoon climbs high into a tree.

Raccoon and heron tracks

THE RACCOON'S FUTURE

Raccoons are not fussy eaters. If one of their foods disappears, they find another. Because of this ability to live even when their habitat and food change, raccoons are very common animals.

In some places they are too common. On Florida beaches, raccoons dig up and eat hundreds of sea turtle eggs. In many cities, raccoons tip over garbage cans and leave a mess.

For the most part, though, people enjoy raccoons and their curious habits.

Glossary

boar (BORE)—a male raccoon

habitat (HAB a tat)—the kind of place in which an animal lives, such as woodland

kit (KIT)—a baby raccoon

litter (LIH ter)—a group of babies born together of the same mother

nocturnal (nohk TUR nul)—active at night

omnivore (OHM nih vore)—an animal that eats both plants and animals

predator (PRED a tor)—an animal that kills other animals for food

prey (PRAY)—an animal that is hunted by another for food

range (RAYNJ)—the entire area in which a certain type of animal lives

23

INDEX